EDITORS DESK

Praise the Lord! Welcome to another issue of Gospel 4 U Magazine. Gospel 4 U is moving forward, thanks to the Lord God who has been faithful, also let me say a special thanks to CLC Bookstore for giving us the opportunity to have the magazine in their store, there is a great move on the horizon and we are following the lead of the Spirit.

We appreciate all our readers and all our contributors that are writing articles for the magazine and I would like to say a special thanks to CLC Bookstore for giving us the opportunity to be featured in their store, God is in the Blessing business and as long as we are in line, we will see the results, there is nothing that can abort what God has started and I would like to help someone reading this today, not because you might be delayed, don't get anxious, don't throw in the towel, God is still in charge.

You are a citizen of Heaven and because of that you have already won, just learn to be patient because the moment you run out of patience then you will quit believing.

Please enjoy this issue and as you read the different articles, I pray that the Lord will deposit a word in your Spirit that will take root and bring forth fruit!

God Bless

Joanna Birchett

MARKETING MANAGER
Joanna Birchett

EDITOR
Cala Allison

ART DIRECTOR
CTS Graphics
Visual Lighting

PRINTING
Good Shephard's Printing

Connect with us via
Facebook ~ Gospel4utv
Twitter ~ Gospel4unetwork
Email ~ info@gospel4u.tv
Website ~ www.gospel4u.tv
Phone ~ 717-685-5191

table of contents
June/July

Gospel 4 U Network where we are dedicated to building the Kingdom of God one reader and viewer at a time
<u>www.gospel4umagazine.com</u>

This Month

ON THE COVER

Fashion Spotlight
Dell Scott
(Page 10)

Out and About With
Ms. Kala
(Page 29)

Additional contributors
Rebecca Rush
Pastor Vanessa Hayes
Prophetess Shirelle Roberts

Pastor Jason Nelson
"Shifting The Atmosphere"
(Page 4)

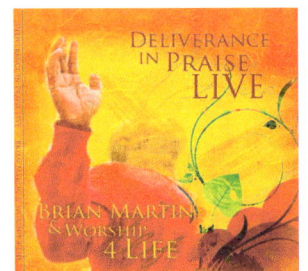

Brian Martin & Worship 4 Life
(Page 19)

Pastor Riva Tims
"Forgiveness"
(Page 16)

Harvest House Restoration Center
1 Year Anniversary

Friday July 12
Starting at 7:00pm

Prophetess Deneen Harrison
The Love Center WorldWide
Baltimore, MD

450 East North Street
Carlisle, PA 17103

Saturday July 13
2:00 – 6:00pm

Apostle Earl Palmer
Brand New Life Cristian Center
Philadelphia, PA

At The Red Roof Inn
Banquet Facility
1450 Pike I81, Exit 52
Carlisle, PA 17015

Sunday July 14
10:00am Service

Pastor Larry Birchett, Jr.
Harvest House Restoration Center
Carlisle, PA

450 East North Street
Carlisle, PA 17103

COME CELEBRATE WITH US
All Events Are Free Will Offering

Recording Artist
Marquita Danzy
Live Performance
Saturday July 13

Hosts:
Pastor Larry Birchett, Jr.
First Lady Joanna Birchett

Pastor Jason Nelson ~ Stellar Award Winner

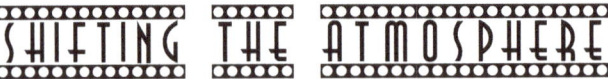
SHIFTING THE ATMOSPHERE

Pastor Jason Nelson thank you very much for taking the time to speak with us at Gospel 4U Magazine. I am going to just ask you random questions so that our readers can get to know you a little bit more.

G4U: I was reading some things about you and I read that you are a PK (Preacher's Kid). What was life like for you growing up in church?

Pastor Jason Nelson: Very interesting. Anyone who is a PK can probably relate to this. You grow up sharing your parents. My father was not only a pastor but he was a Bishop in the organization we were a part of. He also traveled internationally and all of that. We got love and attention but we had to share my dad so there were times when we got it last. I remember there were times in the summer when he would come home at 9 or 10 o'clock and wake us up to go to the park or to play croquet. Just to kind of hang out because he did not have the time to do that on a regular bases like people who were not in ministry. My dad was a great dad and my mom was a great mom they both were great parents. I believe in the hierarchy of relationships it is God, Family, then ministry but in those days it was God, Ministry, then family and we served with them. But it was fun.. We had a lot of fun. My family is very close knit so we laughed a lot. We had great times. The downside is we just had to share our parents with everybody.

PASTOR NELSON TELLS GOSPEL 4 U "I AM A PK (PREACHER'S KID)"

G4U: We often hear horror stories about PK such as rebellion and things of that sort. Did you go through a rebellious stage?

Pastor Jason Nelson: Yeah but mine was kind of a silent rebellion. I am one of those people who is very mission oriented and task oriented so even when I was kind of in a backslidden state I still came to church every week. At that point I was the bass player of the church and I would sing sometimes.
A lot of what I did was outside the confines church hours. I did my share of dirt. (Laugh) and I will leave it at that. (laugh)

G4U: You were called to preach at a young age so even though you may have gone through some things you knew you were called at a young age?

Pastor Jason Nelson: Correct, I heard the call at 17 but I didn't heed it. It was years before I actually gave in to what God was calling me to do. I really had no interest in preaching.

Pastor Jason Nelson

G4U: You grew up in an urban city(Baltimore, MD) how did you not allow the city life to infiltrate you?

Pastor Jason Nelson: We were in church all the time. It's hard to get into trouble when you are always in church. Sunday we had service at 8:00 AM and 11:00 plus Sunday School and then evening service so that was basically all day Sunday. During the week we may have had one or two days off. We had Midweek service, Bible class, choir rehearsals, prayer meetings, Friday night youth services. We were busy. So a lot of stuff some people fell into I never fell into because we were always had something to do. As I got a little bit older some of that stuff just didn't interest me. I wasn't interested in smoking, partying, clubbing, plus I am a little of an introvert so I never really wanted to hang around places that had large crowds. That kept me out of a lot of trouble. As I began to build my relationship with God there was just some stuff that I was like" Naw I am just not doing that." As a result this kept me from falling into the rut that a lot of people fall into. Especially living in metropolitan Baltimore area.

G4U: You have siblings including twin brother Jonathan. Are you identical or fraternal twins?

Pastor Jason Nelson: We are fraternal.

G4U: How was that having a twin brother?

Pastor Jason Nelson: It was great because we always had somebody we could relate to. We had our spats growing up but we could always relate to each other because we were connected. Born on the same day, grew up in the same household and all of that. The difference was Jonathan was a very outspoken extrovert. I was an introvert. I kind of stayed to myself. I was into comic books and video games. He was in choirs and going to church. People could really tell the difference because I never went to church unless I had to. Jonathan went to church all the time. He wanted to know what the new choir songs were and all of that. My brother James, who was a preacher wanted to go to see who was preaching what. James started preaching at 13.

G4U: How did you come about to be the current pastor of Greater Bethlehem Temple?

Pastor Jason Nelson: I was working in the secular realm as an accountant. I felt the Lord kind of pull me to come work for the church to kind of take some of the load off of my father. I left the job against my wife's wishes and started working at the church. I started as chief of staff there and after a few years my father made me the Assistant Pastor. Not necessarily to succeed him but as it relates to the level of authority and I am like " Ok cool" because I didn't want to be pastor. I will serve as your assistant. I only have to preach if you are not there. I was really good with that. Then the Lord started tugging on my heart and I was like " No, No No I don't want to be a pastor. Lord, I am good let me just stick to the singing and I will work at the church. Give it to my brother James. I will serve as his Assistant. That would be good we have a good rapport. It will be great, he is a great preacher. No pressure on me. " But the Lord had other plans. Literally, God sent one prophetic word after another five or six different prophets came to the church and they all prophesied the same thing. One said the older will serve the younger, another prophet came in and talked about Ephraim and Manessiah, Joseph's sons, and how the right hand blessing was placed on the younger son and the left hand was placed on the elder son and then a Bishop from Baltimore came in to preach and literally in the middle of his sermon turned to my dad and said " Bishop, God said it is time for you to get into place but you can't get into your place until Jason gets into his." I'm like, how did I get into this prophecy?

Pastor Jason Nelson

G4U: So your father was the pastor at that time?

Pastor Jason Nelson: Yes and he knew it was time for him to start to transition out and he is torn between myself and my eldest brother James. Then we had a prophet come from Trinidad. I am playing the bass minding my own business. He calls me over and says "God said you are the one to take this church to the next dimension." And I am like, Ok! He must be talking about the next dimension in worship. Then we had a prophet from Australia. She had a prayer line I was in the sound room and my mother came and said "God told me to come and get you and to bring you into the prayer line." Ok how do you tell your mom no? I went and got into the line. I am the last person in line and the lady comes and says "The Lord says you have a Joshua mantle"" I am like you got to be kidding me!" That was like one of the last confirmations. Throughout that process, my wife was very staunchly against it. I seen ministries fall apart because the spouse of the pastor was against the call. So I said "Lord if this is you then you have to turn her heart." This was my fleece to the Lord. Literally in like three months she stop saying things like "Ya'll can do what yall want to do." I remember when she first said "You know what we can do to help the ministry?" She said WE God was definitely turning her heart. Now six years later she is my biggest supporter. She actually has started several ministries in the church. Things are now going extremely well.

G4U: I seen a picture of your beautiful wife and your family; your son and daughter you really have a beautiful family.

Pastor Jason Nelson: Thank you God has been kind!

G4U: Where did you meet your beautiful wife?

Pastor Jason Nelson: We met at church

G4U: Amen! Now just a couple of questions about your singing because you are not just a husband, father, and pastor you are also an award winning gospel singer. Where was the first time you heard your song played over the air? And how did you feel?

Pastor Jason Nelson: I still remember it to this day. I remember exactly where I was. I was at a restaurant called Simone's. I was sitting outside about to go in to get peach cobbler {that's how definitive this moment was} and the radio announcer said "Now we are going to play a song by Jason Nelson" It was a song called 'Don't take Your Spirit' off of my first record. I sat there with my mouth gapped opened like I can't believe my music is being played on the radio! The radio announcer's name is Dwayne Johnson he is a really good friend of mine. He was the first person to play my music on the radio..

G4U: Is it hard for you to maintain all of these different hats that you wear?

Pastor Jason Nelson: It really isn't. God had graced me with the ability to prioritize and a very uncanny ability to tell people no. Some people don't know how to say no as a result they kind of bog down their calendars and things like that. My family is very important to me and I don't want to miss those moments. I like to be there for the significant moments in my kids' life. As well as you can't really pastor a church and be absent all of the time. So I dedicate three- four days a week to just my family and ministry and the rest of the week I travel and do what I can as a singer and itinerant preacher. You must prioritize and realize there are some things that you just can't do.

G4U: Does your children sing or play any instruments?

Pastor Jason Nelson: Both of my children are very musically inclined. They both can sing. My 13 year old daughter has a great voice and my soon to be 7 year old son can sing as well. They love music but I don't know if they want to do music though.

Pastor Jason Nelson

G4U: Does your wife sing?

Pastor Jason Nelson: She can she will probably deny it but she can. (Laughing)

G4U How do you stay grounded and humble?

Pastor Jason Nelson: Family is a very huge key in staying humble because they don't treat me like a star. At home your daddy they don't care that I have won awards or on the radio. They understand what that means but they literally do not care. (Laughing) My kids, my wife, my brothers and my sister they don't care that I am who I am outside of the family dynamics. I have friends who don't care. There is nobody feeding my ego when I am at home.

G4U: So it is only those outside of the home like "Oh wow there is Pastor Jason Nelson!"

Pastor Jason Nelson: Yes and you have to take that with a grain of salt. If you are wise, you will take it with a grain of salt and you are crazy if you believe your own press. I pray quite a bit. I ask God what does He want me to say and what does He want me to do. Humility is the only way to excel from a Kingdom perspective. The Bible says that God resist the proud but He exalts the humble. I have learned that it is not me but it is God's grace on my life that allows me to do everything that I do.

G4U: Tell us about the songs that really have a strong meaning to you. The ones that you sing and can go right into the presence of God when you sing them.

Pastor Jason Nelson: That is a great question. There are a couple on my first record. 'Word Shall Perform' is one of my favorite songs it deals with the now move of God and how by faith we can believe things won't take a long time but that God can accelerate movement. I love singing that song. One of the first big songs that I had is called 'I Shall Live' and I probably say to this day that it takes the most out of me to sing. It is requested quite a bit but a lot of people in the general public do not know that song exists so I am probably going to re-record it again. Then of course you have 'Shifting the Atmosphere' I love singing that because as a worshipper I love being able to invoke God's presence and that is really what 'Shifting the Atmosphere' is all about; bringing God into your current context. 'Nothing Without You' is one of my favorite songs as well because without God in the picture what could we do? How successful could we be? One more song would probably be 'No More Words' off my new album, that song is really based on the heart of a worshipper. You get to a certain point when you are talking about God you run out of words to say. Anybody who has ever been deep into worship, you get to a point where your verbiage doesn't seem sufficient enough and that is why I love that song. It talks about those moments {There are times words failed to describe the majesty of you, So insufficient to really speak of you Lord most of all for you I am awe. It's who you are. There are no letters that fit together to testify. None can describe your love your mercy, that's who you are. To tell of your goodness and your sacrifice. No words that have been heard. So I'll just say you are my God.} I LOVE that song.

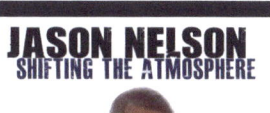

"HUMILITY IS THE ONLY WAY TO EXCEL FROM A KINGDOM PERSPECTIVE."

G4U: Wow! It is really apparent you are not just a singer you are a worshipper. You are not just singing but you are helping people to enter into the presence of God.

Pastor Jason Nelson: Yes, When I got together with my producer I said I want to sing songs that people can sing that would lead them into worship that actually details their life as a worshipper and I believe we captured that.

G4U: What are you doing now? What is the name of your newest CD?

Pastor Jason Nelson: The name of my current CD is called Shifting the Atmosphere. The name of the title song is also called Shifting the Atmosphere. It is available everywhere.. Walmart, Target, Best Buy, iTunes, etc... Right now I am singing and preaching everywhere that God opens the door for me. In August I am going to London for the first time. I am really excited about that! It has been a long time coming. I have always wanted to go. God is taking me not just nationally but international as well. I am just really greatful. My new single is just hitting the radio this week. Called Nothing Without You.

Prophetess Ayanna Moore is a contributing writer for Gospel 4U Magazine. Ayanna is also a Wife, a Mother (Natural, Spiritual, Foster), ordained minister, mentor, author, publisher, and more but the title she is most thankful for is Anointed Servant of the Most High God.

www.the-tstation.com

Readers you can connect with Pastor Jason Nelson via his websites:

Personal: www.jnelsononline.com

Church: www.gbtonline.org

Twitter: pastorjnelson

Thank you so much for taking the time to speak with us at Gospel 4 Ministry. We look forward to seeing your interview with our CEO Evangelist Joanna Birchett. We pray the Lord will continue to bless and elevate you as you humbly worship Him and bring other people into the presence of God. We thank God for who you are in the Kingdom.

Thank you Ayanna

Coming Soon IN the next issue

Look for articles from some mighty women of God
In the September issue of Gospel 4 U Magazine
As 7 women take you there
Teaching you to to Reclaim our identities
Discover our true worth
Overcome challenges and move forward.
These articles will renew, refresh and revive you .
You will be BLESSED!

women of worth

For purchase or information, Please contact Lavette Morant at (215) 900 - 6326

BRINGING THE TREASURES OF THE EARTH TO THE PEOPLE OF THE WORLD

Do you know someone that drinks coffee?

I am sure you do.

If your answer is YES!

We got news for you, try us and you will not be disappointed

The Best Coffee that money can BUY

Let Your Conscience Be Your Guide

By Prophetess Shirelle Roberts

Corporations spend a great deal of money creating jingles, slogans, and images to attract consumers. These schemes attract the lust of our eyes, the lust of our flesh, and the pride of life. Sexual subliminal messages are thrown and delivered to our minds like the morning paper on our doorsteps. Sexual-gratification is the gospel according to the world and has become the new gospel to the church. "If it feels good do it!" If it makes you happy do it. Kraft introduced a shirtless man on their recent TV commercial heralding, "Let's get Zesty". While McDonalds slogan is "I'm loving it". Mountain Dew proclaims, "Just Dew the Dew". And lastly, Nike says, "Just do it". Unfortunately, these images have quite a negative influence within our subconscious. Eventually, they influence our buying behaviors, our lifestyles and even our actions. Everyone knows that "Sex" sells even our children.

The bible does not teach that sex in itself is sin, only when it is exercised outside of the biblical principles of marriage. The same God who instantaneously spoke the universe into existence by the power of his creative word also created sex! (Genesis 1:28) Sex when exercised within the moral boundaries of holiness is one of the most beautiful gifts the Father ordained between a man and a woman. "The two said the Father shall become one flesh" (Genesis 2:4). It literally binds two hearts together into one body. It is such a powerful spiritually binding union, that some of the most anointed people or should I say people in whom we think are anointed are caught in a snare of the most sexually perverted vacuums. Sadly, some apostles, prophets, bishops, elders, pastors, teachers, ministers, evangelists, and laymen alike are finding it a challenge to abstain from sexual encounters while in ministry. Titles are not a camouflage for sin. The real truth is Christianity does not have some magic wand that we can wave over our sin and in a puff of smoke we are delivered. No, no, no! It's the goodness of God that leads to repentance. (Rom2:4)

Nelsons' commentary says it this way, "Deep within man is the consciousness of God, (John1:9) and the sense of what God requires. The conscience of men dwells in the heart acting as a moral regulator of what is right and wrong. The implied meaning of the word conscience is a "knowing within oneself". Since memory and thinking are functions of the heart that is the apparent location of the conscience. The heart is the place where God communicates to man. However continually stifling the conscience renders it inoperative. (1Tim4:2)". In other words, man knows what is right and what is wrong. But if we keep on sinning the heart will become darkened and defiled to the point that we will do what is sinful continually. That is what is known as "having your conscience seared with a hot iron" (1Tim4:2). As saints of the Most High God we must be careful not to engage in anything that darkens our conscience. The danger is, if we continue to suppress the truth in our conscience in unrighteousness, God will abandon us to reprobate minds thereby causing us to exercise uncleanness, fornication, wickedness, greed, envy, murder, deceit, pride, deception, unforgiveness, unnatural affection, and many other works of the flesh repeatedly. So brothers and sisters in Christ let us take careful heed to the deeds that are done in our bodies knowing that they which commit such things are worthy of death. (Romans 1:32). Thank God for the BLOOD!

Fashion MONTHLY

Summer is here Divas! It is a time where you relax, grow, try new things, fellowship, and just EXHALE! It is a time to enjoy, embrace and explore life! It is a time for you to dare, for you to dare to DO YOU!

Make yourself a priority this summer. Sometimes you have to uplift, encourage and edify yourself in order to continue to move effectively in your purpose. Believe me, there are enough accessories this season to have you moving fabulously! Keep in mind, your image directly reveals how you feel about yourself to others and can open the door of opportunity to divinely connect with someone. From hot days to those cool summer nights, there is a candy store of fashion that awaits your wardrobe!

Dell Scott

Summon Your Summer Style

Summer breezes bring power packed color and styles to our wardrobe this season. There are citrus colors such as Nectarine, Lemon, and Lime to bold colors such a Monaco blue and Emerald blowing our way. Sporty dresses let us bring our casual game up to speed, while jumpsuits and rompers let us play around in style. Shortsuits have become the new career chic, while

Peekaboo dresses definitely keep our attention. Striped and chevron print designs in an array of colors and patterns have us waiting for the ready command, while eclectic prints reign supreme this season. Ice cream colored jeans with a pair of heels become our go to look. Don't forget about those lace dresses that let us flow in elegant style and long defining maxi dresses as well. Swimsuits take over the shorelines with colorblock and wild print appeal!

Bold and beautiful is not just for television anymore! That is the motto for summer jewelry. Turquoise selections continue to be an all time classic, while Chunky statement rings adorn our fingers. Stacked bangles, Wrapped bangles and Ornate cuffs become our go to pieces this season. Oversized earrings add defining moments to our fashion this summer, while Hi-polished metal jewelry in all tones, outshine all the rest.

Arm candy packs a punch this summer! From colorful envelope and box clutches to studded totes, you will have a hard time deciding which to choose. Statement sunglasses will allow you see in style and to be noticed a mile away. Metal belts in all shapes and sizes drape our waist and flow while we walk down the street. Decorative summer hats turn up the heat while shielding us from it!

This season's shoes are made to let you strut your stuff, take a walk on the pier with an Eclectic design wedge or show off your botanical flow with a pair of Floral applique sandals. Gladiator sandals are still leading in battle, while a checkered pair of Pointy-toe pumps will have you winning in the boardroom. Go for a Stacked heel or Ankle strapped wedges and sandals for extra appeal!

The bar for beauty has been taken to a new level with the Neon colored hair trend! Loose beach waves and Low ponytails become faves for fun in the sun. Add a floral applique to your hair or wrap it up in a print scarf just for kicks. Nail art is just as bright and colorful as the fashion scene, with neon colors, pearl, crystal, and exotic accents galore. Electric blue eyeliner and bright eyeshadows light up our summer nights while Purple eyeshadow creates the new smoky eye look for this season.

Become super chic in a peekaboo dress and heel. Update your casual work look with a sporty shortsuit and pointy-toe flats. Bedazzle us with your nail art or neon colored streaks on a cool summer night. Rock that print romper with a distinct wedge and some stacked bangles. As you explore the sights of this season, remember you are made in his image, which is "excellence", so let the sun shine brilliantly on your new look!

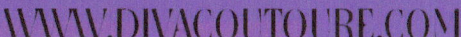

Fashion Consultation, Personal Shopper, Fashion Design Services
Jewelry, Shoes, Accessories, Clothing
(800) 804-0194

WWW.DIVACOUTOURE.COM

The JOURNEY

Rebecca Rush

A Woman of God that desires the power of God to be evident in her life has now birthed forth a ministry that is in high demand and is going forth in the Kingdom, God has placed a mantle on her life for people and no matter what you have been through, she is here to tell you that, you can begin again. Take this journey with her.

My journey first began

My husband and I found out we were expecting a child due to be born on February 1st of 2013…my mother's birthday! Although at the time we were not trying to conceive, we were elated that a baby was on the way! Just when the joy and excitement finally settled in we later found out that we had lost that child and were deeply saddened by what occurred. During the time, it was a very painful and a difficult process that we had to endure but I must add that through it all God was there!

Just when it felt like things were getting better:
In January of this year I believed in my heart that I was pregnant again, and went three and a half months with symptoms, weight gain, and a missed period! Though the tests kept showing up negative, I truthfully thought I was one of those women who had a low hormone level and would show up testing positive for pregnancy later on. I had been back and forth to the doctor and they didn't know what was going on! The whole time was a very emotionally draining process, only to find out months later that there was no baby! After an ultrasound, my doctor finally sat me down and said to me, "you know the mind is a powerful thing." I had what was called a mental pregnancy; changes in my body that happened because of my thoughts and deep desire to be pregnant. I was humiliated and it was then in my moment of despair, that I realized my obsession with having a child was taking over my life. After continual prayer, fasting, and stillness before the Lord, God allowed me to finally experience the peace of God that transcends all understanding.

Something Beautiful Was Finally Birthed:

Throughout my journey of waiting, I've often asked God why my wait seemed to be so long. In the midst of waiting, the Lord finally revealed some of my purpose in this season. I know there are many others who may be asking God the same questions, or experiencing a similar period in their lives. God showed me that the one true way for me to encourage others is through my transparency. I know I shared a lot of details that the average woman would never publicly speak of, but all of it is necessary to my testimony and to give God all the glory! This is why this ministry is so close to my heart, and ultimately so important to me. It was through my pain and struggles that this ministry was birthed. Moreover, I know with God's guidance the ministry will reach many people and help them during their journey of faith, to truly discover their purposeful wait!

Part 2 of The Journey

In the meantime, my husband and I still believe God for the physical **manifestation** of our promise…**children**! Though the journey has been what feels like long and testing, we know that God is going to bless us in His due time. I have learned so much as a result of this wait! My faith has been tested, but in spite of it all, God brought something so beautiful out of it…**Purposeful Wait!**

Psalm 126:5 *"They that sow in tears shall reap in joy.*
6 He that goeth forth and weepeth, bearing precious seed, shall doubtless come again with rejoicing, bringing his sheaves with him."

PURPOSEFUL WAIT - A SUPPORT GROUP

Psalm 27:14 - "Wait for the Lord; be strong and take heart and wait for the Lord."

Isaiah 40:31 - "But they that wait upon the Lord shall renew their strength; they shall mount up with wings as eagles; they shall run, and not be weary; and they shall walk, and not faint."

Purpose - To provide ongoing emotional and spiritual support to individuals who are waiting on God to perform miracles in their lives, based on God's irrefutable promises.

Mission Statement- We believe in empowering others to find their Godly ordained purpose during their season of wait.

About- Purposeful Wait is a non-profit faith based support group that meets bi-weekly to discuss what God says about waiting, whether it be for healing, deliverance, a spouse, a job, etc. The support group welcomes both males & females over the age of 18 who are eager to fellowship with others who are enduring the process of wait. The group will entail a biblical based message, testimonial time, and an open forum.

What stage of waiting are you in:

1) Denial

2) Anger

3) Bargaining

4) Depression

5) Acceptance

These five stages of waiting are very similar to the stages of grieving

Perhaps you thought your period of waiting on God is meaningless and too painful to endure? Or maybe you have allowed anger and resentment to fill your heart because you feel like God is taking too long? You might even have thrown in the towel believing that delay automatically means denial? Or maybe you have finally come to the realization that God's timing is just different from our own. Well, whatever your situation know that God uses our waiting periods as a faith journey. While you are walking this journey of faith, you will need to know what God says about waiting and His promises, as well as hear others' testimonies of God's faithfulness to those who wait on Him…so come out and join us!

Group Information:

When: Meeting every other Monday starting 6/17/13 from 7-8:15 p.m.

Where: Brand New Life Christian Center, 6301 Germantown Ave. Phila, Pa. 19144

Enter on Washington Lane. Meeting room: The Small Sanctuary

Who: Men & Women ages 18 and up are encouraged to attend

Contact: For more information contact Rebecca Rush at purposefulwait@gmail.com or call (267) 540-3136

PHOTOS FROM THE BOOKSIGNING

I WOULD LIKE TO GIVE GLORY TO GOD FOR EVERY DOOR THAT HE HAS OPENED FOR ME, IT'S BY HIS GRACE AND MERCIES WHY I EVEN EXIST AND HE HAS GIVEN ME THE COURAGE TO BOLDLY SAY "DEFEAT WAS AND WILL NEVER BE AN OPTION FOR ME"

SPECIAL THANKS TO MY BEST FRIEND AND HUSBAND LARRY BIRCHETT JR. FOR HIS GREAT SUPPORT IN ALL MY ENDEAVORS, TO CLC BOOK STORE FOR THE GREAT OPPORTUNITY AND BLESSING, TO MY SISTERS, FRIENDS AND ALL THE SUPPORTERS THAT CAME OUT, YOU GUYS ROCK! IT WAS A GREAT SUCCESS.

From Worship To Warfare

By Pastor Vanessa Hayes

The word of God warns us that in this world, we would have tribulations, troubles and fiery trials; therefore, we need to be prepared at all times for what lays ahead. If our hearts are prepared, through intimacy with the Lord, we will not be caught off guard or offended when these things happen. Over the last 30 plus years we have seen a dramatic renewal in the church in the area of worship and spiritual warfare. Accompanying this renewed vigor was a greater understanding and revelation of spiritual warfare and prayer, this new season however requires that we have a deep, intimate relationship with the Lord equips and prepares us to fight the spiritual powers that are responsible for the increase of darkness on the earth.

As I watch the world around us change, as the church changes, our worship has seemingly taken on a new look, sound and feel; I have been concerned about our responsibility is as the worship community in light of the world light growing dimmer and dimmer. It is vital that we understand the type of warfare we are engaged in and what type of warfare is needed. In our Western culture we have turned our worship of God into worship of self, yet the Bible is full of instruction on what God desires from us as we come before Him – which is what worship should be about. What we are witnessing is a challenge to our faith, spiritual passiveness and un-militant approaches to the enemy's plans of destruction. Our worship is characterized by passive non-involvement, intellectualized proposition, and a seeming absence of God in our midst.

Warfare

The Lord is releasing new revelation to His church concerning their power and authority in Him and how to engage in a specific type of warfare against the powers of darkness that have been released in the earth. David was both a worshiper and a warrior. As we look at this life we see a mild mannered, tender hearted shepherd boy caring for his father's sheep. As he grows into maturity and manhood, he shifts into a warrior, a strategic marksman and military might. What happened to David? His worship trained him to hear and be sensitive to God, so that when it was time for him to transition, he was ready for God to use. Throughout the ages the enemy has ceaselessly been working at destroying the body of Christ. He is strategizing against local congregations and has far too often succeeded at poisoning churches and destroying ministers of the gospel. Believers have widely been ignorant of the enemy's schemes leaving them vulnerable to attacks of the enemy, and even becoming the enemy's instruments themselves through sin.

We must learn how to fight in the season; our worship must change from just singing songs to tapping into the realms of the Spirit and pulling down strongholds. The Christian life is the life of a soldier who is constantly at war. He is equipped perfectly, and he knows he is on the winning side. All he has to do is use the weapons the Lord has given him and exercise his authority for the advancement of the kingdom of God. All his actions must be based on his intimate relationship with his Lord and a lifestyle of worshiping and honoring Him.

Pastor Riva Tims

Pastor Riva Tims is living the Majestic Life as a Pastor, for more than fifteen years, a Mother, Motivational speaker, and an Entrepreneur.

Pastor Riva's inner beauty, gentle spirit and passion for Jesus are an inspiration to those who want to know Him. Through prayer, patience and perseverance, Pastor Riva is blazing a trail for God's kingdom and is fulfilling her destiny.

The Maryland native was raised in a Christian home with her identical twin sister, Rená. Excelling in her leadership roles in her church in Maryland, Pastor Riva was elevated through the levels of ordination as a deacon, minister, and elder and eventually she was ordained a pastor.

Pastor Riva has a deep passion for needy and hurting people, out of which a mission for outreach and evangelism evolved. She is the C.E.O. and founder of Majestic Life Institute (MLI). MLI was designed to enhance individuals by delivering quality resources: spiritual, psychological, educational, financial, and physiological. While doing the work of the ministry through MLI, possibly her greatest challenge came when God called her to start a new work after surviving a devastating transition in her life. With much prayer and counseling, Pastor Riva accepted the call and in September 2009, Majestic Life Ministries opened its doors as a local church.

The mission of Majestic Life is to minister, motivate, and mentor members to mature in Christ and maximize their gifts in Him to live the Majestic Life! She is committed to training leaders by hands on mentoring and cultivating. She is also dedicated to the local community through many evangelistic outreach programs.

With humility and generosity of spirit, Pastor Riva helps God's children to lead productive purposeful lives. She is the Co-Host of the "Riva and Dee" TV Show, the Host of the "Glory of Gospel" Radio Program on 94.5 FM, and she has her own health and wellness company.

Pastor Riva openly expresses her greatest joy in life is being a mother of love and excellence for her four children. She devotes most of her spare time to the special needs of her son and children like him born with cerebral palsy. In her quiet moments she enjoys reading, performing arts, history and spending quality time with her children.

**Check out her book
"When It All Falls Apart"
in local bookstores and online**

Forgiveness - The Next Step

Forgiveness is a decision to let go of resentment and thoughts of revenge. The act that hurt or offended us might always remain a part of our life, but forgiveness can lessen its grip on us and help us focus on other, positive parts of our life. Forgiveness can even lead to feelings of understanding, empathy and compassion for the one who hurts us.

It is an act which is done out of obedience to God. Since forgiveness goes against our nature as human beings, we must forgive by faith, whether we feel like it or not. We must trust God to do the work in us so that the process of healing can be complete. Furthermore, forgiveness doesn't mean that we deny the other person's responsibility for hurting us, or minimize or justify the wrong. But it is only through God that we can forgive the person without excusing the act.

Forgiveness is a choice we make through a decision of our will, motivated by His command to forgive. The Bible clearly instructs us to forgive as the Lord forgave us: Colossians 3:13 Bear with each other and forgive whatever grievances you may have against one another. Forgive as the Lord forgave you (NLT).

When we let go of grudges and bitterness we make way for compassion, kindness and peace. When forgiveness is released it leads to: healthier relationships, greater spiritual and psychological well-being, and less anxiety, stress and hostility.

God truly honors our commitment to obey Him and our desire to please him when we choose to forgive. He completes the work in his time. We must continue to forgive, by faith, until the work of forgiveness is done in our hearts.

> "FORGIVENESS IS A CHOICE WE MAKE THROUGH A DECISION OF OUR WILL"

Here are a few steps you can take to walk in forgiveness and freedom in any area of your life.

1) F = Face the facts and recognize that you have anger, bitterness against a person and it is preventing you from living an enriching life.

2) O = Obey God's word and make the choice to forgive yourself and others.

3) R = Recall the offense or situation that made you upset or offended. State aloud: "I fully and freely forgive _____ (person's name) for _____ (list what the person did)."

4) G = Give the benefit of the doubt that the person that may have hurt you is also hurt and they were not intentionally out to hurt you. It is important to separate the "act" from your "identity". Your image in God is protected and can't be changed by anyone. So don't allow emotions or circumstances to interfere with your identity!

5) I = Imagine yourself breaking free and clearly state: I fully and freely forgive _____ (person's name), and I am now released. Pray accordingly.

6) V = Value the experience of forgiveness, the process adds eternal rewards to a person's life.

7) E = Embrace forgiveness as a tool to strengthen your life and the lives of others.

Remember, by forgiving someone, you'll free up space in your heart for more wonderful blessings to arrive in your life, so don't hesitate simply take the next step!

For Booking and more information

Phone: 407-296-8587/321-279-4576

Email: info@majesticlifechurch.com

Website: www.majesticlifechurch.com

Facebook: Majestic Life

Mailing address: 6782 North Orange Blossom Trail, Orlando, Florida 32810

London-Based Brian Martin & Worship 4 Life Complete Groundbreaking USA Tour

By Venice Watson

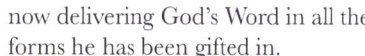

Dateline: London June 13, 2013)

Ministering through music to audiences from Baltimore, MD to New York City, London-based Brian Martin & Worship 4 Life recently completed a triumphant tour of the Mid-Atlantic and Northeast capturing the heart and soul of audiences with a sound that is universal, glorifying God through praise and worship.

Says Brian Martin, *"God has constantly impressed on my heart since we started this journey that the USA is one of the places He wants me to share my music ministry"*

And share they did – From major radio stations like Clear Channel's WCAO Heaven 600 in Baltimore to Bloomberg News Radio in New York, Brian Martin and Worship 4 Life blessed audiences through the airwaves, in churches and Christian retailers like CLC Book Center in Wyncote, PA.

During the 12-day tour, Brian Martin & Worship 4 Life ministered through music in 9 churches in 4 states, including Pastor Donnie McClurkin's Perfecting Praise Church in New York. "We were so graciously received by each church we visited that it is a humbling experience," says Brian Martin. "I believe our music ministry has impacted those people who saw and heard us because of the overwhelming positive response that we received. Everywhere we went we sold out of CDs. During the trip, and since our return to London, we continue to receive feedback about how our music has encouraged and blessed people." That's how we know, by the grace of God, that our music had an impact."

Brian Martin & Worship 4 Life launched their new single "Just For Who You Are" as the flagship song of their Summer 2013 American Tour.

Brian Martin & Worship 4 Life captures the heart and soul of their audience with a sound that is universal and incorporates strong lyrical content with rich musical definition that resonates in the soul.

Brian Martin is a gifted songwriter, arranger, producer and worship leader who communicates God's Word with clarity and conviction. He succeeds at delivering messages that are accessible and challenging. Committed to communicating from a Christian worldview, Brian Martin is now delivering God's Word in all the forms he has been gifted in.

Born on the sunny Caribbean island of Trinidad, Brian came to London at the age of 19 to study mechanical engineering. On the same day he arrived in the UK, he went to church to give God thanks. The message he heard lead him to make a decision to give his life to Christ. Brian knew from very early on in his walk with Christ that he was destined to serve within the music ministry.

In October of 2011, Brian Martin & Worship 4 Life released their 2nd CD, "Deliverance In Praise" in the UK and the USA. The title song, "Deliverance In Praise", a moving worship anthem, impacted Gospel media worldwide garnering radio airplay in the USA and the UK.

Be on the lookout for Brian Martin & Worship 4 Life. They will be returning to the USA this summer. For more information on where to see and hear Brian Martin & Worship 4 Life please visit brianmartinworship4life.com/.

For further information contact:

Vernice Watson
The Artist Company International
9722 Groffs Mill Drive #212
Owings Mills, MD 21117
410-654-6083
theartistcompany@aol.com

TRIUMPHANT FAITH INTERNATIONAL WORSHIP CENTER
WELCOMES YOU!

A Message from the Pastors

We want to give you a warm and heartfelt welcome. We're so glad that you were led of the Lord to visit us here at TFIWC. You know, Jesus said go into all the world and preach this gospel to every creature. Our vision here, is to do just that. It is our desire to save the lost and to make disciples of men and women for the Lord. We aspire to create strong and stable families for the Kingdom of God and to lead people right into their God-ordained purpose. Here at TFIWC we believe that "Ministry is People"!

Our goal is for every believer to have a witness that's undeniable, unavoidable and irresistible. Every Heir of God should be in an atmosphere that allows them to enter into the presence of God in a corporate setting. In this ministry you will experience the freedom of prayer, praise, worship, the Word of God and the fire of the Holy Ghost flowing throughout the congregation. We have said repeatedly, "Lord teach us, to teach Your people, how to love You". We are delighted to say that the ambiance of this ministry is excellence. We strive for excellence in character, conduct and conversation. Excellence must be the integrity that drives this ministry. Before this dying world, that needs Jesus and to have the Body of Christ focused on its mission, we will live right, walk right and talk right. Excellence Is Our Attitude. Remember these words, "Triumphant Faith, Produces Triumphant Living"!

Pastor J Dykeman Brown & Pastor Sandra Brown, Senior Pastors and Founders
5309 Rising Sun Avenue Philadelphia, PA 19120
Main Line: 215.324.7376 | Long-Distance: 877.818.3819 | Prayer Line: 215.324.6787 | Fax: 215.324.5277
Website: www.tfiwc.org | Email: info@tfiwc.org

Weekly Schedule

Sunday
Sunday School — 9:00 - 10:00 am
Corporate Prayer — 9:30 - 10:30 am
Worship Service — 10:30 am
Children's Church — 10:30 am (ages 3-10)

Monday-Friday
New Members' Class — 6:30 pm (Mondays)
Corporate Prayer — 6:00 - 7:00 am
Corporate Prayer — 7:00 - 8:00 pm

Wednesday
Bible Study — 7:30 pm
Adult Discipleship Class — 6:30 pm
Youth Discipleship Class — 6:30 pm

Thursday
Int'l Intercessory Prayer — 7:30 pm

Friday
Friday Evening Service — 7:30 pm
Real Talk (ages 13-17) — 7:30 pm
All Night Prayer — Midnight - 5:00 am

Ministries

Triumphant Faith International School of Biblical Studies (TFISBS) Classes offered during the day and evening! See website for registration and detailed schedule

Triumphant Faith International Youth School of Biblical Studies (TFIYSBS) Classes offered Wednesdays and Saturdays See website for registration and detailed schedule

Marriage Enrichment
Every 1st Saturday at 11:00 am

Men's Fellowship
4th Saturdays at 2:00 pm

Community Center (Food and Clothing Distribution)
Every Wednesday from 10 am - Noon and monthly every 3rd Saturday

"Like" us on Facebook!

Scan to visit tfiwc.org

Zamar International School of Dance

Contact: Erica Griffin or Carol Tyndale
215-324-7376
info@tfiwc.org
5309 Rising Sun Avenue, Philadelphia PA 19120

Our school doors are always open for new students from ages 3-99. Consider if the Lord would have you and/or your children to become students. We hope to see you at the Zamar International School of Dance! God Bless You!

Pastor Sandra Browm
Founder and President

2 Hearts That Beat As One

Marriage Enhancement
PHONE LINE

We endeavor to give you the tools necessary to enhance your relationship.

Log on to this conference phone line every
Wednesday 7-8 PM

Dial 661-673-8600   Access code 926050#

Available To Do Seminars or Workshops
(With Over 29 Years Experience)

Please contact us at
E-mail: TWOHEARTSASONE77@YAHOO.COM
Phone Number: 267-230-2291

GET A COPY OF THIS CD TODAY BY VISITING OUR WEBSITE AT
www.2heartsas1.org
OR CALL 267-230-2291
YOU WILL BE BLESSED

SHAKE IT OFF

Shake off, every weight, every sin

Shake off, every insecurity that lies deep within

Shake off, every hindrance, every distraction

Shake off, every relationship that causes a negative reaction

Shake off, every hurt, every pain

Shake off, every lie that left a stain

Shake off envy

Shake off lust

Shake off un-forgiveness and leave it in the dust

Shake off pride

Shake off conceit

Shake off fear and shake off defeat

Shake off laziness

Shake off procrastination

Shake off self-righteousness and condemnation

Shake off abandonment

Shake off fear

Shake off who left and who didn't care

Shake off your past, no use in stalling

The atmosphere has shifted and your destiny is calling

SHAKE IT OFF!

By: Phaedra T. Anderson

Copyright © 2013 Phaedra T. Anderson. All rights reserved.

INTERNATIONAL HOUSE OF WORSHIP
"STEP OUT THE BOAT MINISTRIES"

PASTOR DWAYNE DAVIS AND FIRST LADY LINDA DAVIS

COME HEAR

RECEIVE

AND ACT ON

THE WORD OF GOD

Ministries In the Church

- MARRIAGE MATTERS
- REAL TALK FOR YOUNG ADULTS
- IRON SHARPENING IRON MEN'S MINISTRY
- WOMEN OF PURPOSE WOMEN'S MINISTRY
- ASHES TO ASHES OUTREACH
- GOD'S LITTLE LAMB NURSERY
- OUT OF THE MOUTH OF BABES CHILDREN MINISTRY

International House of Worship
90 East Shady Lane
Enola, PA 17025

Surplus Building Materials
Save 30-70% on First-Run Products

- Vinyl Windows: $65-$105
- Lighting
- Interior & Exterior Doors
- Large Quantity of Granite Vanity Tops

- Complete Sets of Kitchen Cabinets
- Entry Doors
- Used Kitchen Cabinet Sets
- And Lots More!

The Perfect Place To Start Any Home Improvement Project!

McCarren Supply

717-241-1342

Carlisle, Pa.

www.mccarrensupply.com

Motivational Moment

THE SHIFT

> Isaiah 43:19 Behold, I will do a new thing; now it shall spring forth; shall ye not know it? I will even make a way in the wilderness, and rivers in the desert.

Has there ever been a time in your life you thought you knew where you were going only to have the Lord change Your course? Let me assure you he has not changed his mind concerning you however, there are times along this Journey called life God takes our preconceived thoughts about our destination, removes them, and implements his desired purpose for our lives. This my friend, is called the shift.

Webster defines a shift as a move or transfer from one place or position to another. In exchange for our self Sufficiency he gives us directions to a place we could never reach apart from him. If we are not prayerful we will Fail to discern the season we are in failing to recognize a shift has taken place in our lives. When the Lord commanded the prophet Elijah to go to the brook Cherith it was for a season. Once that season was up the brook also dried up. Gods provision will always accompany the place he has purposed for you and we must have an ear to hear when the Lord has shifted. If Elijah did not shift with the Lord and move to the new place God commanded him he would have found himself in a dry place without God's provision. We must never get too comfortable and familiar with a place that we are not willing to move when God says move. Remembering the purpose of the shift should give us the courage to obey when it seems difficult.

The purpose of the shift is to have us perfectly aligned and positioned for the next level in God. To give him the glory he deserves and to receive all that he has for us.

Maybe you find yourself at the brook of Cherith today. A place the Lord commanded you to go but something has changed. What was once a place of provision has now become a dry unfruitful place. Have you considered the Lord is positioning you for something great? I want to encourage you today. It might look like you Will never reach the place the Lord has shown you but His word will not return void it will accomplish what It was sent to do. Elijah could have gotten so discouraged by the lack of provision and bitter over what he no longer possessed but he remained focused enough to hear the next move of God for his Life. That place miracles continued to manifest in his Life and the lives of those around him. When things begin to look contrary to what you know the Lord has shown you that is not the time to lose hope but to trust him even the more. Being confident of this very thing, that he which hath begun a good work in you will perform it until the day of Jesus Christ. Philippians 1:6

One very important point to remember during this Transition is even though Elijah was in a dry place God supernaturally provided for him. The drought And famine may have been all around him but God's Favor kept him through it all. We may think the Blessing is coming out but God's glory is revealed By going through. If you will trust and praise Him during this shift he will do a new thing in your life and you will never be the same again!

Pastor Rebecca Cooper

Phone: 1800 723-1590

anointedhandsonline.com

ChosenButterfly Publishing LLC
Books that Transform Lives
www.CB-Publishing.com

*...from Conception to Completion
we are with you, every step of the way!*

Do you have a book to write?
Are you a living Testimony of God's
Transforming Power?

Someone needs to hear your story.

Don't put off tomorrow what you can do today.
We'll help extract and publish the words
God has deposited in you.

"This is what the Lord the God of Israel
says: Write the book all the words I have spoken to you."
-Jeremiah 30:2

General contact eMail address: Info@CB-Publishing.com
Ayanna Moore, CEO: Ayanna@CB-Publishing.com

We publish Christian Literature
Fiction & Non Fiction

† Publishing Packages
† Editorial Services
† Professional Writing Coach
...and more!

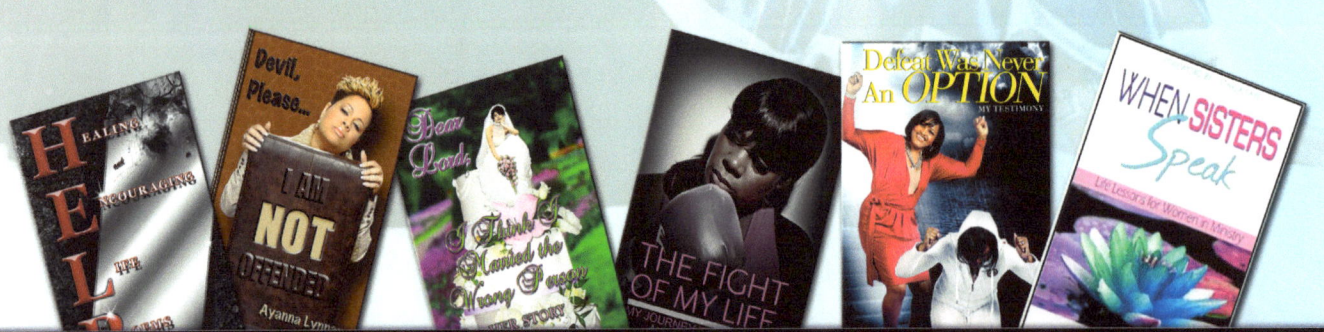

Contact us for a Free 30 Minute Session with our Writing Coach ...You will be amazed at the results!
Web: www.CB-Publishing.com | eMail: WritingCoach@CB-Publishing.com | Phone: (856) 357-3801

Good Food for the Soul of a Godly

As you follow the series of couples' meditations, we hope you will become better equipped to take your part, in kindling the flame that will help married couples grow more in love with God and one another. Let's do the work and nurture that which "God has joined together."

Meditation Thought from Psalm 4:4

Be angry, and sin not.

Meditate within your heart on your bed, and be still.

Disagreements inevitably occur in the lives of married couples. Indeed, we can be honest and admit that small differences, when poorly handled, frequently evolve into full blown arguments. Since both husband and wife are fallen humans, the irritation, frustration, and anxiety related to our unmet expectations are often expressed in angry words and hurtful actions. However, Ephesians 4:26 instructs the believer to "be angry and sin not." In other words, by the power of the Holy Spirit, we should restrain our anger so that we don't act on the sinful thoughts, and we should temper our speech so we build, rather than destroy one another.

In Psalm 4:4 we see David dealing with the issue of anger as he tries to escape the hands of enemies who despise his position as king. While it is not certain from whom David is running, it is clear that the actions of the harsh and unremitting pursuer are causing him extreme grief. In the midst of his troubling time, David humbly casts himself into the merciful hands of God, and advises: "in your anger, do not sin; when you are on your beds, search your hearts and be silent." Thus, David cautions against allowing anger to become a barrier in our relationship with God. It is also clear that even when circumstances provide cause for the anger, we should not let it have mastery over us and lead us to sin.

While David was not referring to marital discord in Psalm 4:4, his words certainly provide wise and Godly counsel for couples who strive to avoid the hidden snares of sinful expressions of anger. If we hear David's advice, we will understand that there is a time when we should stop pursuing our irreconcilable differences and search our own hearts as we sit silently before God. The truth is that most of us spend far too much time probing the heart of our spouse, and too little time praying and inspecting our own. David suggests that we call a moratorium on our fiery disagreements and diligently seek the Lord's enlightenment.

Sinful anger, bitterness, jealousy, etc. are parts of our fallen nature and will automatically manifest unless something is put in place to obstruct the natural course. The answer is to replace our efforts to advance our selfish agenda with an earnest pursuit of holiness, and a desire to please God. When we fill our hearts and minds with the Word of God and prayerful meditations, we interrupt the sinful thoughts that lead to ungodly anger. Remember, the most challenging battle is not from without, but from within.

Rev. Evelyn Barnes has been married for 42 years to Pastor Hubert Barnes of the Star of Hope Baptist Church, located @ 7137 Hegermen St., Philadelphia, Pa. 19135.
Telephone: (215) 332-1130

Continued on next page

The next time we are riddled with blistering antagonism towards our mate, let's consider ourselves at the red light of the conversation. Let's stop, look and listen to God first, and then to one another. Certainly, when we strain to hear and follow the voice of The Lord, He will make our crooked ways straight. My friends, it is in God's divine wisdom and strength that divergent paths of husbands and wives merge and become one. To God be the glory!

Things to Prayerfully Ponder

It is good to have a plan for how you will disagree, even before there is a disagreement. Define what is reasonable and what is outside the boundaries of acceptable behaviors and language in your relationship?

1. It is a good idea to put a bitter conversation "on pause" to give both the opportunity to work on the relationship with God and not the problem. Give yourselves time to gain God's perspective and direction before proceeding.

Final Thought

During an argument, it is always best to spend more time understanding than being understood. When taking a position and forming a response, the ears are far more valuable tools than is the mouth.

© 2013 All rights reserved by Evelyn Barnes

Out And About With Ms Kala ™

"I'm going Out And About With Fred Hammond and Guess What…You're coming with me!"

Hallelujah! My name is Ms Kala, and I'm an actress and Gospel Music Radio Personality who loves to inspire people. I have been blessed withthe opportunity to talk with some of the most inspiring Gospel Artists of our time. I am going to share with you the day that I was blessed with an interview with the Legendary Fred Hammond. **Mr. Hammond shared with me a testimony about the first time he came to know God for himself at age 11 and he shared with me, the gift that his mother gave him that changed his life and hers and helped him to reach the world.** Proverbs 22:6 *"Train up a child in the way he should go and when he is old he will not depart from it"*

One day after a concert in Philadelphia, I met Fred Hammond. I was full of nervous energy and anticipation. I prayed and did some research about his life and I knew what I wanted to ask. I just had one little obstacle, I didn't actually have a scheduled interview with Fred Hammond I just had **"Faith"** ☺

When we got backstage we saw every gospel artist except Fred Hammond. We knew that he was here at the concert but we hadn't seen him yet. He must have come in through the stage door and was in his dressing room. There were some really important people coming in and out of his room so we stopped one of them, and with a big smile on my face I said hello, and asked if I could have an interview with Fred Hammond. I was told, he wasn't taking any interviews right now and to try later. Now, there were some other people waiting for interviews also and they heard what they told us, and they decided to go on about their business. Well, having an interview with Fred Hammond was my business so, I wasn't going anywhere. We stayed and waited, and waited, and waited. Then finally, Fred Hammond's door opened and out he came, he said "Hi you doing" And just as I was about to introduce myself a group of people walked him to the stage. I followed the crowd and watched his awesome performance, stage left. I am an ultimate fan of Fred Hammond's music and I love to dance to it. When I hear some of his upbeat songs I'm liable to break out in a Salsa dance.

After Praising God with Fred Hammond (as he ministered on stage) he walked back to his dressing room and went inside. After about 20 minutes we thanked God for the interview that we were going to have, and knocked again. One of his staff members came out and said "Maybe later". So, I still waited because I had faith. Just then the Lord blessed us with a friend and fellow radio personality who knew Fred Hammond for years, Ms Neicy Tribbett. She was going into Mr. Hammond's dressing room to say hello and she spoke on our behalf. The door opened and we were welcomed in. Hallelujah! It was finally my turn to talk with Fred Hammond. I was full of nervous energy and excitement. With all those feelings I got in front of the camera and sat down on a counter top next to Fred Hammond. With the camera rolling I said "I'm here with Fred Hammond, and I've got a big ole smile on my face" and I let out a big chuckle and he looked at me and laughed too. After that I wasn't scared anymore. The Jesus in him saw the Jesus in me and I forgot I was ever nervous.

The first thing I wanted to talk about was about "The Base guitar that his Mama gave him and how important it was for her to make that investment into his life and into his future."

Fred Hammond responded that it was *"Key"* and that he had a little base guitar when he first got started, that his mother gave him. She said that if he did well with that one that she would buy him a better one. Well, that Base ended up underneath his bed and his mother found it one day and was very disappointed in him. She asked him why he wasn't playing it. And he said "Mom they laugh at me because it doesn't sound good, it's not a real guitar and they laugh at me." After that day Sometime went by, and one day she took him to a really good music store and "the man brought out a Fender Precision, and it cost $413. And she put her head down because she didn't have the money and she said it's a car note, it's basically like a car note. And she went on ahead and signed for it and said. I hope you don't put this one under the bed and I never did…and that Base in turn, not only did it help me reach the world but it helped her retire because of the seed she sowed it retired her. It let her move to Vegas, Atlanta, let her move to be with her kids in Texas and when she had a stroke it put her in the finest nursing facility in Dallas Texas. It means a lot to sow into your kids because you never know when it's going to come back."

His testimony of his mother sowing into his life meant so much to me. I am a mother of two wonderful little girls and I do my best to sow into their lives. It is amazing to be able to have such an incredible impact in someone else's life. Mr. Hammond sharing his story about his mother with me compelled me to share with him stories about my two little girls and how one wanted to play the drums and the other wanted to be a model. While I told him this story I broke into tears. Literally, I started crying during the interview, as far as I was concerned that was not suppose to happen. I'm sure you don't learn that in journalism school.

I just had one more question for Mr. Fred Hammond I wanted to know "The First time he came to know God for himself" He went on to tell me that when he was about 11 years old and his Mother had been going through a rough time after the loss of her husband who was Mr. Hammonds stepfather. He said that his mother had given up on God and that she went silent on God. That she felt bad because the lady across the street who drinks hadn't lost her husband and the other families who cuss and drink that their families were still intact. Then finally one day she told him that they were going back to church and he said "*My mother witnessed to me and that was the first real witness that I had. I couldn't believe how broken I was at 11 years old...I went to her room and I kneeled at her bed and I started crying at 11. And said God I'm sorry I cussed yesterday, that I stole some now or laters.* ***I mean I confessed everything I could confess as a kid and I cried and I didn't know what to do, and I cried and I was so broken. But I didn't realize that was the moment I found God.*** *...I remember that day and I remember how I felt being bad at 11, the curse of sin. ..That was when I really first found God.*"

Thank you Mr. Fred Hammond, what an incredible testimony. I didn't mind waiting, because the half of an hour that he spent with me, would bless my life and touch the lives of thousands of others. What an incredible gift!

To watch this Fred Hammond video and other inspirational videos with your favorite Gospel Artists check out www.outandaboutwithmskala.com

A Special Thank you to Mr. Fred Hammond and our Out And About Team: Juan (Brutha Craze) Baxter, Mark Savage Jr., Erica Brown, and Derrick Woodyard.

Go Out And About With Ms Kala on Praise 103.9FM and www.praisephilly.com on Saturdays from 10am-2pm.

Out And About With Ms. Kala, LLC A Christian Entertainment and Education Company. We offer Fun and Interactive Team Building & Communication Workshops and Inspirational Videos. For more information contact mskalaoutandabout@gmail.com.

www.outandaboutwithmskala.com

Is living healthy hard work?

Of course it is. We don't expect to get something so beneficial for free. By just sitting on your couch all day and watching television, or talking on the phone, you won't miraculously turn into a healthy human being.

Check out these 5 ways that is recommended to work for us:

1. Study the Word of God

2. Eat well

3. Clean up your act

I'm not just talking about physical clutter here. I'm also talking about emotional clutter, as well as psychological clutter. There's a lot of forms of clutter. The most common ones are smoking, alcoholism, drug dependency, etc.

4. Exercise & Walking

The results were amazing. The group who actually walked for at least an hour a day came out healthier and lived longer lives than the other group.

5. Get enough sleep

******Try this for the next 21 days and watch the changes******

www.ingramcontent.com/pod-product-compliance
Lightning Source LLC
Chambersburg PA
CBHW041227040426
42444CB00002B/77